नोट्स फ्रॉम नोव्हेयर

फायरबॉक्स

Made with ♥ on the Notion Press Platform
www.notionpress.com

Dedicated

To our friends, family, and loved ones

क्रम-सूची

क्रम-सूची

पावती (स्वीकृति)

Acknowledgment

With hearts full of gratitude, we at Fireboxx extend our sincere thanks to everyone who made this anthology a reality.

To our gifted authors, your creativity and dedication have breathed life into these pages. Your stories, rich with imagination and emotion, are the heartbeat of this collection. We are honored to have been part of your literary journey.

A special thank you to our CEO, Mr. Akash Gupta, whose inspiring leadership and unwavering belief in this project have been instrumental in bringing this anthology to fruition. Your vision and guidance have been a cornerstone of our success. Your innovative strategies and tireless efforts have ensured that this anthology reaches the hearts and hands of readers far and wide.

Our heartfelt thanks to our Project Manager, Mrs. Aakansha Bhargava, whose exceptional organizational skills and steadfast support have kept us on track and motivated throughout this journey. Your contributions have been invaluable. Your dedication is truly appreciated.

To our compiler, Ms. Prayorshi Mishra, your keen eye for talent and your ability to weave these diverse pieces into a cohesive collection have made this anthology a true masterpiece. Your dedication and passion for literature are evident on every page.

A special thanks to our readers, whose love for stories fuels our passion for publishing. Your enthusiasm and curiosity are the reasons we strive to bring new voices and tales to the world. We hope this anthology brings you as much joy in reading as it did for us in creating.

With warmest regards and deepest thanks,

Fireboxx

1

PROJECT HEAD & COMPILER

2

Aakansha Bhargava

Aakansha Bhargava is an aspiring writer, and BRAVO world record holder, pursuing her passion of writing. Her debut book is Nishabd bol to which she played a role of compiler compiling 22 writers all over India. She has participated in 30+ anthologies as a co author. She is obsessed with books since kindergartens. She is always ready to outcast her opinion as a leader.She is having leadership qualities as she can lead with her skills. She has taken an initiative for Animal Welfare to treat stray animals for their food and Safety.

क्या फ़र्क है

क्या फ़र्क है जो मुझे वो शाम याद नही

तेरे सा थ पिया वो जाम याद नहीं

पर मुझे याद है तेरा मेरे लिए फूल लाना

और अपने हाथों से मेरे बालों में लगाना

और ये भी की सड़क के किनारे हाथ तेरा पकड़ना

कोई चोट लगने पर अपनी बाहों में जकड़ना

और इक शाम गले से तेरे लिपट रोई थी मैं

बेफ़िक्र ज़माने से हो ,तेरे कांधे पर सो ई थी मैं

तो क्या फ़र्क है जो मुझे वो शाम याद नहीं

|तेरे साथ पिया वो जाम याद नहीं

हाँ याद है जब नज़रों से डराया था तूने मुझे

मैं बस तेरी हूँ ये एहसास कराया था तूने मुझे

और ये भी की सादा सा कुर्ता पहन मैंने खुद को सजा या था

और तेरा नाम ले अपनी हर ग़ज़ल को फरमा या था

कैसे कह दिया कि प्यार नहीं मुझे तुझसे

तेरा लगाया मुझ पर ये इल्ज़ाम याद नहीं

क्या फ़र्क है जो मुझे वो शाम याद नहीं

तेरे सा थ पिया वो जाम याद नहीं

3
Tour to psyche

Listen,
I think I have to take you on a tour to my psyche....

M feeling dizzy, feels like something is controlling
me.....

My premonitions made me feel like I'm in another
world....

I sometimes wonder, why I'm so detached from this
body?

I don't know the exact reason why,but I do know that
the feeling is eating me up inside......

I'm feeling like uncomfortable, unfulfilled, seems like I
don't know my path, my wrong and rights...

Constantly searching for a place where my heart once
living peacefully, where I waggle like butterflies, and
chirp like hummingbird....

It's all hollow now, a sense of failure occupies the

place where ambition once lived...

Searching someone, who make me feel less alone in
the moment, who is not cruel, the void.... Particular

void begins to consume me again and again.....like a

small scared kid,who is constantly seeking for a hug,
It's just I feel disconnected right now....

So dear world, stop pretending like an alibi, if I'm
blaming you for the cause....

Knowingly or unknowingly life is going at dead ends,
everything is now feeling lighter and warmer and
warmer.......

4
Akash Gupta

Akash Gupta, the founder of Fireboxx Entrepreneurs Pvt. Ltd., is a visionary young entrepreneur dedicated to turning his ambitious dreams into reality. He completed his B.Tech from Jain University, Bangalore (2016-2020) and went on to earn his MBA from AIMIT (2020-2022). Akash launched Fireboxx in 2019, driven by his relentless passion to become one of the most successful entrepreneurs. He is not just a dreamer but a tireless achiever who sacrifices sleep to overcome daily challenges and pursue his entrepreneurial aspirations with unwavering determination.

आख़री ख़त

दिन सुरमई सा लगता है
जरूर उन्होंने आंखों में सुरमा लगाया होगा ||

और बहुत रोशनी है चांद मे आज...
शायद उसके हूर बनने का समय आया होगा ||

यह चांद की रोशनी जगमगा रही है...
जरूर उनके आंगन में भी खुशी आई होगी ||

मगर इतनी मायूसी क्यों है आकाश में...
जरूर उनकी आंखों में मायुशि से आई होगी||

इतनी सुहानी रात में यह बारिश कैसे हो रही है?..
शायद उनकी आंखों से आंसू आए होंगे ||

दिन सुरमई सा लगता है ...
जरूर उन्होंने आंखों में सुरमा लगाया होगा ||

यह बारिश की बूंदे मिट्टी को महका रही है ..
जरूर उनके हाथों में भी मेहंदी लग रही होगी ||

दिन सुरमई सा लगता है ...
जरूर उन्होंने आंखों में सुरमा लगाया होगा ||

अब नहीं थम रहे मेरे आंखों से आंसू क्यों?
अब नहीं थम रहे मेरे आंखों से आंसू क्यों?

शायद उसके पिता ने उसका कन्यादान कर दिया होगा ...
अब मेरा शरीर इतना ठंडा क्यों पड़ रहा है...
शायद उसका सिंदूरदान भी हो गया होगा ||

अब उठ रही होगी उसकी डोली उसके घर से ...
और यहाँ हमारे जनाजे का इंतजाम हो रहा होगा ||

दिन सुरमई सा लगता है ...
शायद उन्होंने आंखों में सुरमा लगाया होगा ||

5

Prayorshi Mishra

In the enchanting tapestry of emotions, Prayorshi Mishra emerges as a modern soul trapped in the delicate intricacies of an old-school heart. Her quill dances gracefully on the canvas of paper, weaving tales of her innermost feelings. In moments of vulnerability, she seeks solace in the timeless art of writing, confiding in her pen pal when emotions find no other refuge. With each stroke of ink, she paints a portrait of resilience, patiently awaiting the dawn of her own 'elayne'—a chapter where she can sculpt the contours of her life with unbridled freedom and unrestrained passion.

The Longest Night

That night didn't seem to end

but there was nothing left that could be mend.

Definitely, we've come a long way

forever vows changed into alimony pay .

Painless is to say we didn't try

countless nights gifted us swollen eyes,

and they ask did you even cry?

But, to inculpate them would be right?

Lows were always concealed , all they saw were highs.

Still wonder what was missing

felt it was a beaut hill top,

realised when we started slipping.

Again, not that we didn't try to resort,

but we kept on falling,

perhaps we lacked each other's support.

It's been three years

feels like it happened yesterday.

Maybe it was not wrong,

and maybe it was meant to be.

But is it easy to stand in the dock?

and witness your whole world changing from "we" to

"she" .

6
चल दिए

हमने पूरी उम्र मांगी थी

तुमने एक शाम दी और चल दिए

हमने तो आगाज़ सोचा था

तुमने अंजाम समझा और चल दिए

हमने वक़्त के साथ वक़्त बिताया उस वक़्त के इंतज़ार में

तुमने एक पल इंतज़ार न किया और चल दिए

ये कैसी मोहब्बत,

कि हमने ये पलकें बिछा दी

उन नज़रों के दीदार में

और जब हम महफ़िल में आये

तुम महफ़िल छोड़ कर चल दिए

7

CO-Author

8
Aditya Singh

I am Aditya Kumar Singh, a student at Shri Ramswaroop Memorial University, Lucknow. I am a poet by heart; I love to express my feelings and expressions through poetry. I write on topics like love, emotions, heartbreak and social topics in our motherland Hindi. My parents, Mrs. Reeta Devi and Mukesh Kumar inspire me a lot for this. They help me a lot in this journey and my inspiration for writing is my poet friend DEV. At last, one line about me is.."अपने खाली वक्त में अपने खाली पनो को लिखा करता हूं"

सुनो,
कैसी हो जान........

शायद ये कहने का हक खो दिया है मैंने।
पर खुदा कसम तुम्हे हद से ज्यादा प्यार किया है मैने।

तुम खुश रहो हमेशा खुदा से बस यही दुआ करता हूं।
मैं आज भी वही पागल लड़का हूं,और आज भी मैं तुमपे ही मरता
हूं।

तुम तो शायद भूल भी गई होगी ना मुझे।
तुम तो अब याद भी न करती होगी मुझे।

तुमने मुझे एक सपने की तरह भुला दिया है।
घर के इस शहजादे को, किसी फ़कीर की तरह रुला दिया है।

अब ये लड़का बंद कमरे में सहमा सहमा सा रहता है।
हर पल तुम्हारी ही तस्वीर से बाते करता रहता है।

तुम्हारी याद में हर रात अपने आंसुओ से अपने तकिए को भिगोता है।
ये दुनिया को हंसाने वाला लड़का अब बंद कमरे में सहमा सहमा सा रहता है।।

• 17 •

9

Agrini Mishra

Agrini Mishra, a poetess at heart trying to navigate life through verses of my own. My poem, "Loneliness," is a reflection of navigating the challenges of fitting in, embracing solitude, and ultimately finding beauty within isolation. This writing of mine is my experience with my cherished companion "Loneliness", capturing emotions that resonates with heart of many

Loneliness,
Something I never wanted to be a part of,
And none of us want to be a part of.

I met loneliness,
I met it when I came second in the class,
I met it when I was told I am not cool enough,
I met it when I had my first heartbreak,
I met it when I was told that I am a misfit,
But you know when I met it for real that time I was broken.

Living in a strawberry world— seemed so beautiful and bright,
The girl who used to stand in the corner crying over a toffee —
entered the world
of wrong and right.

I walked on my pace not knowing what was wrong and what was
right,
And that shit really screwed me tight.

It made me meet something I never knew about,
I always thought I would do the best but gradually I just fell out of
step .

I was never alone but was lone,
I had friends and family but deep down I was still unknown.

I always looked for something but I didn't know what,

Is it humans or me? was a thought battle that I always fought.

I met loneliness—
A feeling: not of despair,
People always mistake it not for good, but this is where I came to know
something big was out there.

It made me meet an unknown feeling,

A feeling that solved my question of right and wrong and I felt quite belonged.

Being lone I felt that ease,
People call it shit but it was my real peace.

I often questioned myself that what I was about ,
And it taught me that I was born to stand out

From being strangers loneliness turned into my lover,
Whenever I had fears it gave me a cover.

I proudly can say that loneliness is my lover,
And this journey from strangers to lover is the only cover.

10
Akshita Mishra

I'm Akshita Mishra, a wordsmith weaving tales in the loom of language. With ink-stained fingers, I compose verses that echo the heartbeat of life. My poetry, a symphony of emotions, invites you to stroll through the garden of contemplation. My words dance between the profound and the mundane, inviting you to explore the tapestry of existence through the lens of my poetic vision. Join me on this literary odyssey where every line is a whispered conversation with the soul.

।। प्रेम राग ।।

खवाब जो खवाब से हैं
खवाब ही खवाब में वो उलझे हैं
प्यार से टटोल के देखो
खवाब तो वो प्रेम के हैं।
जान के अनजान बनी मैं
प्रेम के दरिया से
जो खवाब में है, जो जबान पे है
पर लफ्जों में ना आ सके हैं।
तरसती हूं मलहम को मैं
धीरे–धीरे से लहज़े को मैं
वेदना को लपेट के
खुशियों को उभारने हैं।
अल्फाजों को बटोरती मैं
शब्दों में तोड़ती मैं
ना जाने कैसे लिखूं ये एहसास
जो प्यार के सागर से हैं।
अरे। सुकू न को ढूंढती मैं
हर वक्त हर मोड़ पर
कं कड़ विश्वास के बटोरती मैं
जो फरयाद के धूल में खोए से हैं।
डूबी हुई रहती हूं मैं
दिल – दिमाग के गुफ्तगू में
इकरार किसका हो , इंकार किसका हो,
जब दोनों एक ही समान सा सोचे हैं।
लफ्जों को समेटती हूं मैं
मोतियों में पिरोती मैं
खाली से मन को मकान और
एहसासों के संसार से छत बनाने हैं।

मंद –मंद मुस्काती मैं
खुद से बात करती मैं
ख्वाब को सुन कर देखो मेरे
वो तो अपने ही धुन समझाते हैं।
ख्वाब जो ख्वाब से हैं
ख्वाब ही ख्वाब में वो उलझे हैं
प्यार से टटोल के देखो
ख्वाब तो वो प्रेम के हैं।

11
ARSH SRIVASTAVA

A technically creative person who mostly write around realistic fictional situation.

रो -रो के दिन को रात करेंगे

यादों में जब मुलाक़ात करेंगे

खड़े हैं इसी इंतज़ार में हम

साथ बैठेंगे कभी तो बात करेंगे

रास्ते में कोई अंजान आ गया

हर किसी के मनोभूमि में ज्ञान आ गया

पहले तो मदद करने को ,

रुक जाते थे लोग

अब सबके दामन में स्वाभिमान आ गया

अपनी गिनती कि न आशिकों में शुमार कर बैठे

हम भी एक फरिश्ते से प्यार कर बैठे

और कोई बुलाता तो ना जाती वो

पर खुदा भी एक नायाब दुआ की पुकार कर बैठ

12
Jai Srivastava

I'm Jai Srivastava, a student at Shri Ramswaroop Memorial University. I'm an artist at heart, using words to craft soulful poems primarily in Hindi. My dedication to this art form is unwavering, and I'm passionate about delving into themes of love, care, and the depths of human emotions, including feelings and fears. I find solace and joy in expressing these sentiments through my poetry, channeling them into pieces that resonate with others. My commitment to the language and the emotional depth it allows me to explore is a constant source of inspiration in my creative journey.

"ख़्वाबों की राह"

"दो लफ़्ज़ों से ख़त्म हुई वो कहानी,
आज कई सवालों को बुन रही है।
तेरी ख़ामोशियों ने जाहिर कर दिया कि,
इश्क़ हमारा मुक़द्दर नहीं।
आज भी जवाबों की तलाश में,
न जाने कितनी रातें भटक चुका।
फिर भी ये न जान सका कि,
बेरहम तो मंज़िल है, सफ़र नहीं।

ज़रा ज़रा इन आँखों को,
आंसुओं की कीमत समझा रहा हूँ।
ज़रा ज़रा मैं टूट चुका,
फिर भी इश्क़ की दहलीज़ संभाल रहा हूँ।
फिर क्यूँ, फिर क्यूँ हमेशा तुम आगे बढ़कर नहीं आती हो।
सब सच मालूम होते हुए भी एक लफ़्ज़ कहने से कतराती हो।

गुनाह बता सकती अगर तुम मेरे तो,
गुनहगार मैं ख़ुद को ठहरा देता।
इन हाथों में महज़ इश्क़ से भरे काग़ज़ नहीं होते,
एक ख़न्जर होता और अपने इस दिल पर वार कर देता।

अरे सुनो,
हार कर दुनिया जहाँ से मैं तेरे क़रीब ही तो आया हूँ।
कुछ अक्षर इश्क़ के बख़ूबी चुनकर मैं लाया हूँ।
तुम इजाज़त दो अगर तो मैं कुछ तुमसे कहना चाहता हूँ।
नहीं नहीं, ये फूल किसी और के नहीं,
अरे बाबा, तुम ही रखो,
मैं तो तुमसे इश्क़ जताने आया हूँ।

थक चुके हैं अब ये क़दम ज़िंदगी से,
अब दो पल का ही सही, आराम बन जाओ तुम।
थम चुके इन होठों के लफ़्ज़ सारे,
अब महज़ दो अल्फ़ाज़ों से बयाँ हो जाओ तुम।
कितनी नाराज़गी है तुम्हें मुझसे जो अब ऐतबार नहीं करती,
मैं बुलाता रहता हूँ मगर तुम हो कि एक बार नहीं सुनती।

खैर, अब बातों से तुम कहाँ मान जाओगी,
जाओ जाओ, देखता हूँ कितना दूर जाओगी।
लौट कर आना हो तो बाहें हमेशा खुली हैं तुम्हारे ख़ातिर,
तुम रूठ-रूठ कर मुझसे कितना प्यार जताओगी,
बस करो, बस करो, अब कितने ख़्वाब दिखाओगी।"

13
Dr. SAKSHI GOSAVI

Dr. Sakshi Gosavi. She is a doctor by profession. She loves to write, sing and dance. She is a co-author of many books and a part of many anthologies. A girl with big dreams who want to achieve her goals and become a noble doctor to help needy people.

आखिरी सफर

मुद्दतें बीत गईं तेरे इंतजार में,
ये इंतजार आखिरी है।

सफर आखिरी है, दगर आखिरी है।
मोहब्बत से देखो, नज़र आखिरी है।

आज कल कुछ उखड़े से हो,
क्या हमसे फिर रूठे से हो,
चलो माना लेते हैं तुम्हें एक बार, इस बार मानना आखिरी है।
आज तुमसे बात करने को जी चाहता है,
तुम्हारी बातों में खो जाना चाहता है,
इसी बहाने तुम्हें ज़रा जी भर कर देखने की आस है।
तुम्हें देखकर खो जाना आखिरी है।
चाहत आखिरी है, प्यारी सी वो मुलाकात आखिरी है।

आज शिकायत है बड़ी तुमसे,
क्या गले से लगाकर कह दूं? दिल में भरे मेरे जज़्बात क्या तुम्हारे सामने रख दूं?
जज़्बात आखिरी हैं, शिकायत आखिरी है, इबादत आखिरी है।

कितनी ही ग़ज़लें लिख दी हैं तुझपे,
ये भी है लिखी, मगर आखिरी है।

14

Dr. Tilak Dixit

Dr Tilak Dixit is a practising doctor in government service in Rajasthan. He has been part of 90 plus anthologies some of which have been part of world record certification at different levels. He writes in a metaphor as he believes that metaphors are bridges that connect two or more emotional atmosphere Hope you feel it

प्रेम

जो प्रेम करे वो वाणी से सींचे
जो ही प्रेम करे वो रहे माटी के नीचे

जो प्रेम करे वो करे श्यामा का ध्यान
जो ही प्रेम करे श्यामा रखे उनका ध्यान

जो प्रेम करे वो करे क्षमा श्यामाए
जो ही प्रेम करे वो गाए रमा रमाए

जो प्रेम करे भाव के पीछे
जो ही प्रेम करे नाव को खेंचे

जो प्रेम से सुने
जो ही धरती का आधार बुने

जो प्रेम करे आसूं से
जो ही प्रेम करे जिज्ञासु से

जो प्रेम करे वो भी संत
जो ही प्रेम करे वो बन जाए अंत से अनंत

• 34 •

वो हर प्रेम को हरे जाने
वो हर प्रेम हरी को ही जाने

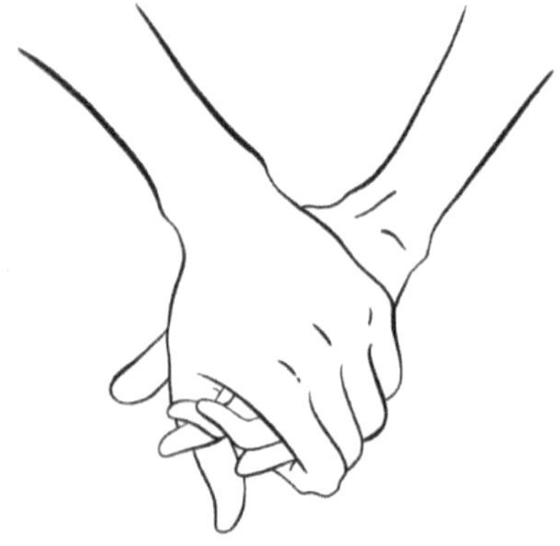

15
MOHA PANDEY

I'm Moha. A blossoming writer and a reading enthusiast who's growing with diction and fiction everyday. When I'm nowhere to be seen, you can find me curled up in my blanket with a murder mystery novel in my hand or cooking pasta because why not. Hope these lines bring a smile on your face as you move ahead with your day and life. Pleasure, with love.

Only SHE creates

The heaven created her and then shivered with a
magnificently cold sweat,

When she came down, a wonderful creation from the
above for mankind to ever get.

The superpowers she has are nowhere to be compared
with anyone else,

She can love with no limits, she nurtures and affection
is all she sells.

But her sales are made with no profit motive, they're
free of cost,

She can heal and make you forget that it is cold when
all you can see is frost.

She is a female, not only human but all of the females
to ever exist,

She was born to create all the beautiful creatures that
the earth consists.

She carries a life in her for different periods with utter
protection and care,

If anyone says that there is a wonder as fantastic as
this,
then it would be unfair.

The lioness raises her cub and so does the cow with her

calf,
All the females are empirically strong and they

prove it with a lovely laugh.
I admire the superpowers a woman has and I'm so

proud to be one,

This is just a pump for all the awesome females who
have left no task undone.

16
Muskan Gupta

I'm Muskan Gupta, a passionate writer on a mission to spin tales that stir the soul and ignite the imagination. With a love for storytelling coursing through my veins, I embark on literary adventures, exploring the depths of human emotion and the vast landscapes of imagination.

Journey Within

I kept on finding solutions

For the problems I didn't know

I knew I wasn't happy

Seeking all around highs for my lows

In the midst of all my searching,

I lost sight of what's within.

Chasing fleeting satisfaction,

Yet the emptiness grew thin.

I sought solace in distractions,

In the noise that drowned my mind.

But beneath the surface turmoil,

Lay the answers I'd yet to find.

So I paused amidst the chaos,

Listened to my heart's faint call.

In the stillness, found the courage

To embrace myself, flaws and all.

No longer seeking outwardly

For what only lies inside.

In acceptance, found my freedom,

In my truth, I now abide

17
MUSKAAN YADAV

Myself Muskaan Yadav from Rewari{Haryana}.I do love reading novels and dowriting poems, stories as well. I am glad tohave an opportunity to write in this anthology.

हक(अधिकार)

अपने हक अपने अधिकार अपने अस्तित्व के लिए लड़ने का पूरा हक है तूझे।
घर हो या बाहर हर जगह अपने हक के लिए बोलने का पूरा अधिकार है तूझे।
आज वो हर काम जो एक लड़का कर सकता है
वो हर काम करने का हक है तूझे,
उसकी तरह जीने की आज़ादी है तूझे।
खेल-कूद , पढ़ने - लिखने हर चीज़ का हक है
तूझे।।
जब कोई तुझे लड़की कह कर तुझ पर रोक लगाए
उसे उस बात का जवाब देकर आगे बढ़ने का हक है
तुझे।
लक्ष्य सामने है तेरा उससे पाने का हक है तूझे,
अपने हर सपने को पूरा करने का अधिकार है तूझे।
जब लड़कर इन सब बातों से आगे बढ़ना सीख लिया तूने,
तो समझ ले कि जीत हासिल कर ली तूने अपने लक्ष्य को पाकर,
तो समझ ले कि अपनी जीत का , अपने अधिकार,
अपने हक को हासिल कर जीत का परचम लहरा दिए तूने।।

18
Pannaga Shree B S

A writer, swimmer, singer, artist, designer and sportswoman
rolled into an engineer.

Crushed

Four. That is the number of fails I have gotten in tests and exams in all of high school and college put together. And not a single one of them had much of an impact on the final results. With a streak like that, it became almost habitual for me to try something and succeed at it, albeit with a few minor setbacks, if that. That streak stayed for a considerable amount of time. I practically never failed at anything for as long as I can remember. Owing to this seemingly long-running luck or success, I never factored in the possibility that maybe I wouldn't get what I wanted when I started something. I didn't have a lot of expectations, but at the back of my mind there was this voice that said, "It'll all work out". I hate to accept it, but I have listened to that voice more often and in way more situations than I should have. That voice is dead now. I don't know if it was true desire or if I had gotten caught up in the trend when I started preparing for an incredibly difficult exam a few years ago. Initially I had no expectations, which is my default setting. But as days turned weeks and weeks turned into months, that voice got louder and more obnoxious. Irrespective of what I said out loud, deep down I believed that I would get into the top university for the program I wanted and that I would cruise through and emerge with flying colours. And getting through the exam and the program became something I actually wanted. I didn't just sit by and hope. I made time and did the work. I was studying when all of my friends were enjoying their weekends. I didn't attend any family get-togethers. Most of the money I spent went into papers, pens, and printouts. I sacrificed a whole lot of my time to work on preparing for that exam. I didn't eat out as frequently as I used to before. I took precautionary medicines just in case I showed any flu symptoms and they mistook it as COVID. I refused to meet any of my close friends because of the fear that one of them might give me an infection or because that 1-2 hours would be better spent brushing up on concepts I wouldn't need in the real world.

Surprise, surprise, I didn't clear it. One whole year of preparation, anticipation, anxiety, sacrifice, dedication, and a bunch of other words I can come up with - They all went down the drain with my horrible marks. I didn't accept defeat. I gave it a second shot and failed again. Needless to say, my self-confidence had considerably gone down. I decided to take a break because I was getting tired of telling people that I did not get through. I prepped even harder than before but that all-assuring voice? It had lost its vigour. The break seemed to drag on forever. It felt like it lasted for more than a year, as I had intended it to. One evening, a few weeks before the exam, I was watching a sitcom and was laughing out loud at some joke I'd heard a million times. I was munching on some of my favourite snacks and both of those were well-deserved considering that I had just completed a revision of my favourite section of the syllabus. It was not too hot, not too cold and I was extremely comfortable on the couch. And then suddenly, the thought of failing a third time crossed my mind. And in a matter of seconds, the thought took over. That was all I could think of. The positive voice was nowhere to be found. I spaced out and my mind was buzzing with the same thought playing backwards and forwards a hundred times. I started to feel a headache coming on and clutched my head. A few seconds later, I broke down crying. The frightful sobs turned into weeping which then ended with me crying out loud and gasping for breath. I could not stop. I could not bring myself to stop. I couldn't move and I sat there, wailing at the thought of another failure for what I reckon was a whole hour. After I calmed down a bit, I vowed to myself that whatever the outcome of this attempt was, I would take it and move on. This would be my last shot at something I had dreamt of for years. Over the next few weeks, I experienced more episodes like this, on the couch, in bed early in the morning just after waking up, on the kitchen floor while trying to cook something, and every time I washed my face. I had sworn off all social media and I stayed away from people in general because I wanted this to be it, for it to be my shot at getting what I had wanted for a long time. I failed, again. It broke something in me. I couldn't take it anymore and so, for the first time in my life, I gave up trying. My spirit was crushed.

19
RAKSHITA BHARDWAJ

I Rakshita Bhardwaj , believe that poetry is a powerful tool to express the complexities of life. It has the ability to capture the essence of a moment, to freeze time and immortalize emotions. My writing is inspired by the world around me, the people I meet, the experiences I have, and the emotions I feel. Through my poetry, I hope to create a connection with my readers, to evoke empathy and understanding, and to spark a conversation about the depth of our hearts and minds.

Fantasizing Death

Death would be so beautiful
To have all your loved ones together
To have all of them to finally be there
To have all of them to cry for
Just like you cried for them
To feel your importance
Death would be so beautiful
To have patience
To have silence
To have no tomorrow
To have no worry
To have no emotion
But just yourself
Death would be so beautiful
I want it
I need it
I beg for it
I lived it
I am living it
But may be that somepart
Which is alive is killing the gem of it
Gratefully someday I'll find it
I wish it to be the
Next day
Next hour
Next minute
Next moment
I wish i was so lucky
Death would be so beautiful
To be wrapped up
To be remembered for
I would love to have it
I want it

I need it
My beautiful death.

20
SAMAY CHANDANI

Amidst gears and graphics, I'm an engineer by trade, Yet in words' music and verse, my passion cascades. At twenty-one, a soul woven in poetic hue, Where engineering meets the beauty of prosaic view. I'm Samay

It's a love story!

Every lover talks about the moon and the stars but among those billions of stars in the universe. Which one is closest to the moon? Which one is darling to the moon? Hey my name is Samay and I am here to talk about love, the way I define it. Let's talk love... So the question is which star is darling to the moon?The answer is the star which is closest to the moon. Matter of fact, we all are darling to the one we are closest to. So you must have got a word to say, the answer is very logical, very scientific. The Sun is the star closest to the moon and we all know this. But how the sun and the moon are lovers? I'll answer this shortly priorly a fact that sun is not the only star and the moon revolving around this globe is not the only moon existing but the sun and the moon are closest to each other in terms of distance and it's nothing to be proved. We all are close to someone and we show then our love, but how? Now that's very difficult to answer. Right? Some show love by care, some by gifts, some by affection, some by deep talks, some scold you when you are wrong, It's love! They just wanna show that you mean someone to them. They entitle you, they love you.This has many answers depending upon situations, people, perspectives etcetra. Coming back to the sun and the moon How the sun shows its love to moon? Science answers everything and that's the reason I love it. Science and philosophy too are lovers^_^ We see the moon, mostly crescent; complete on full moon nights and no moon on new moon nights. Does the moon gets replaced daily? NO. So what happens? And the moon has no light of its own right! Then how is it visible? The sunlight is the answer. We see the moon when the sun sends its love to the moon, let's call it sunlight. The moon reflects it and marks its presence. The sun makes the moon realise its self worth when it hides itself in the dark. That's what makes sun a truelover. That's what is expected from a lover, to support you to mark your presence. That is we call a partnership right? Now everyone must be expecting theirpartners to do something like that. But it's not a one way thing.Now moon shows it's love back? To be honest... It doesn't. So is the sun a one sided lover or is the moon mean? Either of the two isn't true. They are truly in love with each other. Well it's not necessary for the moon to give a favour to show its love. It's enough for the sun if the moon means it. Love my dear is not an agreement with mutual favours. It's all about supporting each other whenever in need. Here intentions matter alot. Be the sun in your partner's life show them their vibrance by reflecting your own. No demands, no expectations; And feel free to ask If you need support. But you need to say it or better ask it cause you being the sun, your moon owes one. And for sure moon will be there for the sunwhenever the sun is in need. Find your moon and be the sun to, It's foreveryone; keep loving ♡

love story

21

SAUMYA MEHROTRA

I'm Saumya Mehrotra, a student at Shri Ramswaroop Memorial University. I'm just like a weaver who weaves the emotions, the thoughts, sentiments In words...I know the art of writing soulful poems which can heals the broken soul and motivate them to move forward...for me , poetry is an ocean of emotions in which thousands of feelings with up and downs can express in just a couple of words....I'm passionate about this wonderful craft in which I can express the sentiments in which allows me to explore more with the words which can heals from the depth.

खफ़ा क्यों हो

खुद ही पहल कर दो
इस कदर खफ़ा क्यों हो
बेवजह जिद के पीछे
कोई रिश्ता बुरा क्यों हो

माना मेरी पसंद अलग है
तेरी ख्वाहिशें जुदा है मुझसे
अब तेरी पसंद का रंग भला
मेरी जुबां पर क्यों हो

मन - मुटाव जायज़ है
दो लोगों के बीच
सोच अलग है दोनो की
इस बात पर झगड़ा क्यों हो

बात करने के लहज़े
और भी हैं कई
हर बार नीम सी कड़वी
अपनी जुबान क्यों हो

बिन रोए भूख मिटती नहीं
नन्हों की भी
मर्ज़ बताए बिना भला
दवा कोई क्यों हो

अपनापन रखो ना औरों से
माँ -बाप के सगे रहो
जो धरती का होता नहीं

उसका फिर आसमान क्यों हो

22
Sonalika Mishra

I'm Sonalika Mishra and I'm a student of MSc 2nd year from Lucknow University. Writing and drawing are my hobbies.

School Life

वो स्कूल की सुनहरी यादें

वो मॉर्निंग प्रेयर में लेट पहुंचना और फिर टीचर्स की नजर से बचकर निकलना

वो लंच में ड्यूटी न करने के हजार बहाने बनाना

वो कैंटीन का एक समोसा जिसमें होता था 6–7 दोस्तों का हिस्सा

वो बिना आउट पास के कॉरिडोर के चक्कर लगाना और फिर पीटी टीचर से डांट सुनना...

वो स्टेयर्स को गॉसिप्स का अड्डा बनाना... वो पनिशमेंट में ग्राउंड के चक्कर लगाना...

वो मार्च पास्ट न करने के हजार बहाने... वो छोटी-छोटी बातों पर झगड़ा... वो हाउस कैप्टन की नजर से बचकर यहां वहां भागना..

वो बैक सीट पर बैठकर लंच के पहले लंच करना..

वो फ्री पीरियड में दमशरास और अंताक्षरी जिसमें दो हिस्सों में बंट जाते थे सभी

वो दोस्तों के ग्रुप जो अब केवल ग्रुप फोटो में साथ है...

वही थे जिंदगी के सबसे खूबसूरत पल जो अब सिर्फ यादों में जिंदा है ...काश फिर से लौट आते वो पल.. काश फिर से लौट आते वो पल..

23
TANYA

I'm Tanya. A literary magician who weaves words into spells that transport readers to enchanting realms. With a pen I tried to transform ordinary sentences into extraordinary adventures.I craft tales that seamlessly blend maturity and mirth leaving readers both enlightened and entertained. Get ready to embark on a journey through the whimsical mind of someone who believes that a day without writing is like a day without laughter -unthinkable and utterly dull.

मंज़िल-एक उम्मीद

आज भी एक उम्मीद में जी रही हूँ...
उस एक सवाल का जवाब ढूँढ रही हूँ॥

न जाने क्या छुपा रखा है ज़िन्दगी ने मेरे लिए..
उसके एक इरादे को जीने के लिए..
दिन रात मर रही हूँ॥

कितनी अनकही बातें समेटे ख़ुद में..
बस चल रही हूँ॥

कोई मुझसे मेरी मंज़िल न पूछे...
मैं मुसाफ़िर, बस भटक रही हूँ॥

इस रात और उस चाँद को पता है मेरे राज़...
वरना भीड़ में तो मैं बस हंस रही हूं॥

24
Tisha Gupta

Hey , I'm Tisha Gupta. A creator of words of emotions, basically I wrote poems in hindi because according to me people connect easily with hindi language and it is easy to convey the message in hindi and I love to write in hindi .

यूपी में है क्या ?

यूपी में है क्या ?

तो सुनो जरा,

यहीं बैठे राम है यहीं बैठे श्याम है ,

अयोध्या में है राम मथुरा में हैं श्याम,

और काशी में कर रहे शिव विश्राम ||

और तुम कहते हो कि यूपी में है क्या?

तो जरा भ्रमण करो और पाहुंचो नीमसर ,

आ रहा कुंड में पानी कहां से पता लगाओ जरा ;

अरे याह रहस्य कोई ना जान पाया कि वह पानी आया कहां से?

रहस्यों से भरा है यूपी और तुम कहते हो यूपी में है क्या?

दिन में रहते लखनऊ में और रात को करते रखवली अयोध्या की, वाह हनुमान भी तो यूपी के हैं |

वाह हनुमान भी तो यूपी के हैं ||

मिथिला से ब्याह कर अयोध्या आयी वाह सीता मैया भी तो यूपी की है ,

कृपा बरसाने वाली राधा भी तो हमारे बरसाने की है और तुम कहते हो यूपी में क्या है?

गंगा ,जमुना ,सरस्वती मिलती है जहां वह संगम भी तो प्रयागराज यूपी में है |

लव कुश का जन्म हुआ जहां वह वाल्मीकि आश्रम भी तो यूपी का है ||

सीता मैया ने बनाई रसोई जहां चित्रकूट भी तो यूपी का है|

अक्षय वट और परिजात वट जैसे चमत्कारी वृक्ष भी तो यूपी के हैं ||

और तुम रहते हो यूपी में है क्या ?

बताने बैठे तो बहुत कुछ है सुनते सुनते थक जाओगे तो जरा अब यूपी के बारे में कुछ कहने से पहले भ्रमण करो यूपी का और तब कहना कि यूपी में है क्या ?

ख़तम हुई बात भक्ति की आते है अब देश भक्ति पर,

क्रांति की पहली गोली दागी मंगल पांडे ने गोली भी तो मेरठ की थी |

1857 में उठी वो तलवार पुरानी थी वह झाँसी वाली रानी भी तो यूपी की महारानी,

जहां जन्म लिया सदर पटेल ,भोपाल कृष्ण गोखले ,डॉक्टर राम मनोहर लोहिया और चन्द्रशेखर आजाद जैसे वीर जावनो ने,

वह मिट्टी भी तो यूपी की है |

जो जिला आजाद हुआ सबसे पहले अंग्रेजों के चंगुल से वो बलिया भी तो यूपी का है ||
और तुम कहते हो यूपी में है क्या?
और तुम कहते हो यूपी में है क्या?

25

UMAIR KIDWAI

As a student at Shri Ramswaroop Memorial University, my nameis Umair Kidwai. I write poetry, mostly in Urdu, because I'm anartist at heart. I have an everlasting commitment to this art formand a passion for exploring themes of love and human emotions,including anxieties and feelings. I take great pleasure and comfort in using poetry to channel these feelings and createworks that speak to other people. In my creative path, mydedication to the language and the emotional depth it permitsme to explore serve as a constant source of inspiration.

ग़म

आगाज़ से ही मुझे दो तुम अंजाम का ग़म
कुछ नाम का है
तो कुछ काम का ग़म
मोहब्बतों को मार दे इल्ज़ाम का ग़म
टूटा दिल ही जाने
ढलती शाम का ग़म
कुछ प्यार का ग़म
तो कुछ यार का ग़म
जो दुनिया में न रहा
उसकी याद का ग़म
जो सवाल ही न किया
उस जवाब का ग़म
इस जिंदगी में ज़िंदगी के बाद का ग़म

26
VIVEK HOTWANI

As a seasoned businessman navigating the world solo at 40,
Living a life and enjoying the melodies at lord Shiva's city
Varanasi. A poet in pursuit of beauty, crafting stories with every
rhyme. **Jai Bholenath!!**

माँ

माँ के बिना संसार नहीं।
माँ के बिना संस्कार नहीं।
माँ के बिना इस जीवन का,
कोई अस्तित्व नहीं, आधार नहीं।

माँ शक्ति है, माँ भक्ति है।
माँ स्वरूप है महामाया का।
बालक तो सूखा पेड़ है,
बिना माँ की छाया का।

माँ की परिभाषा
शब्दो में लिखी नहीं जाती।
बिना माँ की ममता के
ये जिंदगी जी नहीं जाती।

माँ आस्था है।
माँ विश्वास है।
कठनाई में भी शक्ति का आभास है,

माँ अगर पास है।।

27
VIVEK SAINI

I am Vivek Saini, a poet who weaves heart- touching verses that resonate with emotions. With the stroke of my pen, I paint landscapes of feelings, capturing the essence of the human experience. Each poem is a journey through the depths of emotions, inviting readers into a world where words dance with sentiment. Join me on this poetic odyssey, where emotions find expression in the artistry of language.

आँखों का तारा

गमो कि बहती धारा मे वो...
एक सुकून भरा किनारा था।
लाखों की भीड़ थी वहा..
पर वो एक्लोता था जो हमारा था।
हा माना बेजुबान था वो..
हा माना शब्दो से अंजान था वो..
वो जैसा भी था हमारी आँखों का तारा था।

Summary

Notes from Nowhere is a mesmerizing anthology that brings together an eclectic mix of poems and stories from a diverse array of writers, capturing the essence of human experiences in both Hindi and English. This collection is a journey through the landscapes of the heart and mind, offering readers a profound exploration of emotions, thoughts, and dreams.

In this anthology, you'll find tales that transport you to distant places, immersing you in the beauty of the mundane and the extraordinary alike. Each story is a window into different worlds, where the characters' lives unfold with grace, struggle, and triumph. The poems, with their lyrical beauty, delve deep into the soul, touching on themes of love, loss, hope, and resilience.

The writers featured in Notes from Nowhere hail from all walks of life, each bringing their unique voice and perspective to the collection. Their works are a testament to the rich tapestry of human experience, reflecting the diverse cultural and linguistic heritage of our society. From the bustling streets of cities to the quiet corners of rural life, these pieces offer a glimpse into the myriad facets of existence.

Notes from Nowhere is not just an anthology; it is a celebration of storytelling and poetry, a testament to the power of words to connect us, heal us, and inspire us. Whether you are seeking to be moved, entertained, or enlightened, this collection promises to be a treasure trove of literary gems that will stay with you long after you turn the last page.

Immerse yourself in "Notes from Nowhere", and discover the magic that happens when talented writers come together to share their innermost thoughts and stories with the world.

www.ingramcontent.com/pod-product-compliance
Lightning Source LLC
Chambersburg PA
CBHW031500150726
47990CB00007B/2822